Thrive in Year One: The New Agents' Guide to Success

By Annette DiResta

Copyright

© 2025 by Annette DiResta

All rights reserved. No part of this publication may be reproduced, stored in a retrieval system, or transmitted in any form or by any means—electronic, mechanical, photocopying, recording, or otherwise—without the prior written permission of the publisher.

ISBN: 9798992921618

Published in the United States of America

Date of Publication: May 29, 2025

Dedication

To my mom, Diana, whose resilience built a legacy. You've given me strength, perseverance, determination and "will there's a will there's a way" attitude. Whenever we considered making a risky move, you would always respond "do it." Thank you for being a role model as a shrewd investor, living debt free and living a lifestyle of exercise and wellness.

To Brooke and Trevor, my heartbeats since the day you were born, my greatest cheerleaders, and the biggest blessings of my life. Thank you for loving and supporting me unconditionally. Also for being patient with your very imperfect mom. I couldn't have asked nor prayed for better children.

To Eddie, my brother, who has always managed to keep a positive mindset despite walking through decades of hell. Thanks for getting me in the best shape of my life for the Paradise Cup, training at Waikiki World Gym and the Honolulu Club…I will be driving behind you as you jog home from the gym.

To Rita, my sister, scuba diving in the Caribbean and our trip to Medjugorje was the pivotal point that rekindled my spiritual journey and not too long after our return, my rededication to Jesus.

To every new agent chasing their dreams.

Preface

Thriving in your first year as a real estate agent is raw, real, and relentless. This book is a blend of fiction based on experience and real case studies. This story details how my brother Eddie stumbles and rises, felt my sister Rita's steady guidance, and carries our mother Diana's legacy of grit—from Korea's ashes to a tip-jar empire.

This book isn't theory; it's a lifeline—a Thrive Cord of nine strands forged from my family's victories, scripture's wisdom, and stories of agents who turned pain into profit.

These strands—courage, perseverance, gratitude, resourcefulness, focus, identity, collaboration, endurance, and connection—guide you through year one's chaos. You're not alone in fear, rejection, or feeling overwhelmed.

My mission?

To help you weave your cord and stand tall with a story of triumph by year's end.

Let's begin—your first step awaits.

Table of Contents

Introduction: Weaving Your Thrive Cord – Eddie's shaky start and the promise of nine strands.

Chapter 1: Facing the Fear – Courage over comfort conquers doubt.

Chapter 2: Embracing Rejection – Perseverance turns "no" into strength.

Chapter 3: Redefining Success – Gratitude values small wins as divine seeds.

Chapter 4: Starting Small – Resourcefulness grows little into mighty.

Chapter 5: Finding Focus – Focus carves clarity from chaos.

Chapter 6: Carving a Niche – Identity crowns your unique lane.

Chapter 7: Building a Team – Collaboration doubles your haul.

Chapter 8: Staying the Course – Endurance reaps harvests from setbacks.

Chapter 9: Nurturing Relationships – Connection blooms gold from roots.

Conclusion – Eddie thrives, the nine strands repeat as your lifeline.

Call to Action – Practical steps to ignite your year one.

About the Author – Annette's story and credentials.

Acknowledgments – Gratitude to those who shaped the journey.

Glossary – Key real estate terms for new agents.

Index – Themes, scriptures, and case studies.

APA Citations – Validated references.

Introduction: Weaving Your Thrive Cord

On June 12, 2024, the sun sank over a San Francisco cul-de-sac, casting amber hues. My brother Eddie stood on the porch of his first listing—a modest $800,000 condo—his hands trembling as he fumbled with the lockbox, its clank piercing the evening's calm. With $187.43 in savings, his dream of thriving as a new real estate agent teetered after six months of effort. Fear flickered in his eyes—would he fail before starting?

You might feel this too: heart pounding, palms sweaty, doubting your strength.

My vision? You thriving in your first year as an agent.

My mission is to weave your Thrive Cord—nine strands of lessons: courage, perseverance, gratitude, resourcefulness, focus, identity, collaboration, endurance, and connection. Drawn from real case study victories and timeless wisdom, these strands, reinforced by scripture, form a lifeline proven by agents who've triumphed.

Let's weave your cord, starting with your first bold step.

Chapter 1: Facing the Fear

The first strand of your Thrive Cord is COURAGE.

On June 12, 2024, a San Francisco evening bathed a cul-de-sac in amber light, vibrant yet unforgiving. Eddie stood on the porch of his first listing—a $800,000 condo—his hands shaking as the lockbox jammed, its clank cutting the quiet. His savings, down to $187.43, mocked him from his phone's screen. Sweat beaded on his forehead; the bay's breeze failed to ease the panic tightening his chest.

This was his final chance to thrive as a real estate agent, or he'd return to a call center job he'd left six months earlier. Fear gripped him—failure, inadequacy, abandonment—threatening to choke his dreams. You may know this fear: heart racing, doubting your worth, wondering if God's left you.

Joshua 1:9 (NASB) counters: "Have I not commanded you? Be strong and courageous! Do not tremble or be dismayed, for the Lord your God is with you wherever you go." Written around 1400 BC, this captures God's charge to Joshua after Moses' death, facing Canaan's giants (*Joshua 1:1-9*). Fear was real, but God's presence fueled courage, echoing Abraham (*Genesis 28:15*) and Christ (*Matthew 28:20*). Courage is trusting God's nearness when you shake.

Eddie believed a lie: God abandons you in fear. *Joshua* reveals the truth: God is closer than your next breath, equipping you. Fear calls you to lean into His presence, not hide. This shapes **Courage Over Comfort**: **Act despite fear, trusting God's strength**. Fear shrinks when you move with Him. Courage comes from faith, not fearlessness.

Case Study: Zdenek Tronicek – The FSBO Flip (Pomona)

Zdenek Tronicek stood on a dusty Pomona street in late summer 2020, the heat pressing against his skin like a heavy skillet on high flame, his savings drained to a faint whisper and his wife's doubts ringing in his ears like a fire alarm. Fear coiled tight in his gut—failure loomed, a storm cloud ready to burst. Then he spotted it: a faded "For Sale By Owner" sign swaying in the dry breeze, creaking on rusted hinges like an old gate. His boots crunched over gravel, each step kicking up a puff of earth that mingled with the sharp, biting tang of citrus from nearby groves, a scent that stung his nostrils and woke him up. His hand trembled as he scribbled a note, the pen's scratch loud against the oppressive quiet, and slid it under the door, the splintered wood warm and rough under his fingertips. Days later, his phone buzzed—the seller's voice rasped through, desperate, an investor drowning in credit card debt with no lifeline but Zdenek's offer. He hustled, the escrow office thick with the smell of ink and stale coffee, the papers rustling as he closed the $450,000 deal, pocketing a $6,000 commission that landed like cool rain on parched ground. "I thought I'd crash and burn," he said later, sweat still beading on his brow as he recalled the moment, "but courage was acting through the shakes." By 2021, he'd cooked up $190,000 in earnings, a feast from that first terrified step.

Eddie's hands shook as Rita stepped closer. "Fear's real, Eddie, but God's closer," she said, echoing Diana's escape from Korea in 1951, bombs roaring. Eddie twisted the key—the lockbox snapped open. Relief warmed him as buyers arrived. His open house drew 14 buyers, selling the condo for $825,000 in late June 2024, netting $12,375 (Bay Area MLS, 2024). His cord tightened, courage woven in. Courage starts with one bold move, not zero fear

Chapter 2: Embracing Rejection

The second strand of your Thrive Cord is PERSEVERANCE.

On July 3, 2024, fog cloaked a San Francisco cul-de-sac in damp chill as Eddie slumped on the porch steps. His first cold call ended with a curt "Not interested" and silence, the sting burning his cheeks. His savings hovered after a gas fill-up, rejection sinking like salt air. Rita strode from her office, her day trading chaos in her veins, seeing his sagging shoulders. Eddie rubbed his face, wondering if every door would slam shut.

Rita recalls their mother Diana's early U.S. days—landlords sneering at her thick Korean accent, their curt refusals biting like a bitter winter wind through her thin coat, yet she pressed on, marrying her GI despite the chorus of family's "no." She'd waitressed through it, her feet aching on diner floors, tips clinking into that coffee jar. "'No' forges you, Eddie," Rita says, her tone honed by critics' jabs at her early trades, sharp and unyielding. Romans 5:3-4 fuels her point—Diana's tribulations birthed perseverance, shaping her character to buy that first home in Fountain, Colorado with its damp-earth smell. Eddie's slammed doors are forging his character too, tempering him for the long haul.

Rejection hits new agents hard, making you question your fit, whispering you're a failure. Eddie felt it, believing God punished him with each "no." *Romans 5:3-4 (NASB)* counters: "We also exult in our tribulations, knowing that tribulation brings about perseverance; and perseverance, proven character; and proven character, hope." Written around AD 57 (*Romans 1:7*), Paul's words to a persecuted church show rejection as a forge, building strength through God's love (*Romans 5:5, Hebrews 12:2*). Rejection builds character for success.

Eddie's lie was that rejection meant God's disapproval. *Romans* reveals: Rejection refines you, shaping hope. Each "no" builds your cord. This forms **Push Past "No"**: See rejection as a forge, trusting God's hand. Perseverance leads to "yes."

Case Study: Jason Barry – The Door Knock Deal (San Diego)

Jason Barry stood in Rancho Santa Fe under a sun beating down like a broiler on full blast, his knuckles raw and stinging from rapping on 50 doors. Paint flaked off warped frames, drifting like ash in the still, dry air, while sprinklers hissed a faint mist that kissed his flushed cheeks with a teasing coolness. Each "no" landed like a slap—homeowners' clipped voices cut sharp as a knife through warm butter, their eyes cold and dismissive. The scent of eucalyptus tingled his nose, a faint promise in the heat, but fear whispered he'd never break through. He kept going, sweat trickling down his spine, until door 47—a grizzled man paused, his gravelly grunt softening as Jason pitched, words tumbling out fast as boiling water over a stove's edge. The $300,000 condo listed, the escrow papers crisp and cool in his hands as he signed, sold in a blink, the commission tasting sweeter than fresh-cut lime on a parched tongue. "Every 'no' stung like hell," Jason said later, wiping sweat from his brow with a calloused hand, "but it led to that 'yes'—the one that launched me." Now with $5 billion in career sales, he credits those early slams for his steel. (RealTrends, 2024).

Eddie's cheeks burned, but Rita knelt: "Rejection forges you." Diana endured sneers—he dialed again. A voice said, "Tell me more." Relief swelled; Rita's faith fueled him. The call led to a $650,000 listing, closing for $9,750 on July 15, 2024 (Bay Area MLS, 2024). His cord grew stronger. Each rejection hones your edge—keep knocking.

Chapter 3: Redefining Success

The third strand of your Thrive Cord is GRATITUDE.

On July 20, 2024, a kitchen bulb flickered as Eddie scrolled Instagram, dwarfed by million-dollar closings glaring—champagne, Ferraris—while his modest condo listing a pebble in a sea of glittering gold. The fridge hummed, his chest hollow, success out of reach. Rita stirs Diana's kimchi stew on the stove, the spicy steam curling upward like a prayer, stinging her eyes with its fierce red heat. She recalls their mom's first duplex—warped floors creaking under her sneakers like a groan, mildew wafting dank and sour from peeling walls, yet its $50 monthly profit glowed like an ember in the dark of her single-mother nights. "Small fed us, Eddie," Rita says, precision in every stir, the wooden spoon steady in her hand. Zechariah 4:10 rings true—God rejoiced in Diana's tiny start, a starter home that grew into a legacy feeding three kids; Eddie's condo listing is his ember too, a spark the Lord delights in.

New agents wrestle with comparison, feeling small, believing God favors the big. Eddie bought this lie. *Zechariah 4:10 (NASB)* counters: "Do not despise these small beginnings, for the Lord rejoices to see the work begin…" Written in 520 BC (*Zechariah 1:1-7*), this celebrates Jerusalem's humble temple rebuild, echoing David's sling (*1 Samuel 17*). God delights in small wins.

Eddie thought God ignored his ember. *Zechariah* shifts: God rejoices in your small steps. Success is obedience, not size. This shapes **Value the Ember**: Trust God's joy in modest wins. Gratitude strengthens your cord. Small steps build lasting success.

Case Study: Beckie Nielson – The Social Spark (San Diego)

Beckie Nielson stood on a San Diego bluff in 2021, the Pacific breeze whipping her hair like a whisk beating cream, the salty tang coating her lips as she steadied her phone to film a $600,000 listing reel. Eight failed offers had left her raw—big wins felt like distant stars twinkling mockingly, her phone's screen a dim flicker against the crashing waves below that roared like a packed dining room. She hit record, the sunset blazing orange across the horizon, her voice trembling over the surf's thunderous pulse. Uploaded, it exploded—likes piled up like foam on the shore, the views a tidal wave that swept a buyer in, their footsteps crunching on the hardwood as they toured. The escrow office hummed with the buzz of printers spitting out contracts, the check's ink still wet as she clutched it, tasting victory sharper than lemon zest on a fresh catch. It closed in 30 days, a small spark that lit her path. "I thought small moves were nothing," Beckie said later, sand still gritty between her toes as she stood on that bluff, "but that reel sparked it all—it was my beginning." By 2023, she'd closed $12 million (AgentAdvice, 2024).

Eddie stared at his phone, but Rita's spoon clinked. "Small fed us," she said, Diana's legacy in her voice. He posted his listing, a call came: "I love it." Gratitude warmed him—he was seen. The condo sold for $675,000 on August 1, 2024, earning $10,125 (Bay Area MLS, 2024). His cord glowed. Small wins plant big roots—start there.

Chapter 4: Starting Small

The fourth strand of your Thrive Cord is RESOURCEFULNESS.

On August 10, 2024, Eddie sighs at the kitchen table, the weight of empty pockets pressing like a cold marble slab on a prep counter after paying his real estate licensing and MLS dues. His bank app showed $162.19. Rita entered, light catching Diana's tip jar. She points to the jar on the shelf—tips once clinked into it, a chime that turned into a shack with walls that sagged like overcooked dough. Eddie rubbed his temples, Diana started with pennies—could he? "Start where you stand," Rita says, the relic gleaming like a beacon in the dim light. Matthew 13:31-32 fits perfectly—Diana's mustard seed of a rental, small and unassuming, sprouted a tree of stability that shaded her kids; Eddie's small start, even with no cash, can branch out into something mighty too.

New agents face empty pockets, believing God won't provide without wealth. Eddie felt this lie. *Matthew 13:31-32 (NASB)* counters: "The kingdom of heaven is like a mustard seed… the smallest of all seeds, but when it has grown it becomes a tree…" Spoken in Galilee, 30AD (*Matthew 13:1-3*), Jesus shows faith's power (*Judges 7, 2 Kings 4*). God multiplies the small. Small investments grow big returns.

Eddie thought he needed money to win. *Matthew* shifts: God grows what you have. Little is enough. This builds **Resourceful Roots**: Use what's in your hand, trusting God's multiplication. Resourcefulness roots your cord.

Case Study: Elisa Covington – The Budget Boost (Riverside)

Elisa Covington gripped a hammer in Riverside's blistering summer of 2012, the sun searing her skin like a griddle on high, sweat beading and dripping as sawdust stung her nose with its dry, woody bite. She had no cash—just a $250,000 short-sale fixer-upper, its walls sagging under neglect, the air thick with mold's sour reek that clung to her throat like a bad batch. Her arms ached as she pounded nails, the clang ringing sharp through the still heat, plaster dust coating her tongue with a gritty tang. She flipped it for $350,000, the $100,000 profit hitting like a cool splash on a scorched day, the escrow office's hum a sweet lullaby as she signed the final papers, their edges crisp against her calloused fingers. The scent of fresh paint lingered on her clothes as she walked away, a new foundation under her feet. "I thought I needed millions to even start," Elisa said, her voice steady as she brushed dust from her jeans, "but that little deal built me—nail by nail, sweat by sweat." By 2015, she'd flipped $3 million (New Silver, 2023).

Eddie eyed the tip jar as Rita nodded. "Start where you stand," she said. He grabbed a free flyer, called and pitched a lead. Hope flickered—a $700,000 listing closed for $10,500 on August 25, 2024 (Bay Area MLS, 2024). His cord sprouted. Little grows mighty with work—begin now.

Chapter 5: Finding Focus

The fifth strand of your Thrive Cord is FOCUS.

Eddie juggles scripts and cold-call lists at the kitchen table, chaos mounting like a kitchen rush gone wrong—papers scatter, his voice hoarse from half-spoken pitches. She recalls Diana's hands calloused from bartending and waitressing tables to signing deeds. "One thing, Eddie" she insists, "have razor-sharp focus," cutting through his clutter like a cleaver through bone. Proverbs 16:3 guides her point—Diana committed her knocks to God, each step setting her path firm as concrete; Eddie's focus can solidify his plans too, turning chaos into order.

The feeling of being overwhelmed buries new agents, blurring paths, suggesting God's plans fail. Eddie believed he had to chase all leads. *Proverbs 16:3 (NASB)* counters: "Commit your works to the Lord, and your plans will be established." Written in the 10th century BC (*Proverbs 1:1-7*), Solomon's wisdom shows focus as God's order (*1Kings 6, Exodus 13:17-18*).

Eddie thought he needed everything. *Proverbs* shifts: God clarifies when you commit one thing. This forms **One-Tool Focus**: Master one skill, trusting God's order. Focus sharpens your cord. One skill brings clarity.

Case Study: Tracy Tutor – The Expired Revival (Los Angeles)

Tracy Tutor stood in a Brentwood fixer, dust motes swirling like steam in the dim light, a $700,000 expired listing mocking her with its six-month silence, its stale musk heavy as old grease. The feeling of being overwhelmed clawed at her—her partner's "Pick one" echoed from a stale sushi lunch after losing three deals. She could chase a dozen leads or focus. She staged it, her heels clicked decisively on the scratched hardwood, each step a drumbeat of intent. The fresh paint's crisp, clean bite sliced through neglect, stinging her nose as she staged it—cushions plump as risen dough, lights warm as a hearth's glow. Her pulse raced, a familiar rush from open houses, as buyers toured, their murmurs soft against the walls. It closed in 45 days, the commission check crinkling in her hand, its weight a triumph sweeter than caramelized onions melting on the tongue. The escrow office smelled of toner and promise, a quiet victory hum. "I thought I had to do it all at once," Tracy said, her voice echoing in the now-empty house, "but one tool—focus—sold it, turned chaos into cash." focus wins every time." Ignoring distractions, closing for $10,500 in 45 days. By 2024, she'd hit $50 million (Hollywood Reporter, 2023).

Eddie's papers fluttered, but Rita cut through: "Pick one thing." He booked a showing—clarity settled. The $750,000 sale earned $11,250 on September 20, 2024 (Bay Area MLS, 2024). His cord sharpened. Focus sharpens your edge—pick one tool.

Chapter 6: Carving a Niche

The sixth strand of your Thrive Cord is IDENTITY.

On October 1, 2024, Eddie leaned against the kitchen counter, drained, calls to condos, mansions, and rentals unanswered. Coffee lingered stale, savings at $140 after groceries. Eddie tries every lead at once, drained like a line cook on overtime, his energy fizzling as calls go unanswered. "I'm nobody special," Eddie muttered, lost in the crowd. Rita fires back, "Specialize."

New agents feel invisible, believing God made them generic. Eddie bought this lie. *1 Corinthians 12:4-5 (NASB)* counters: "Now there are varieties of gifts, but the same Spirit… varieties of ministries, but the same Lord…" Written around AD 55 (*1 Corinthians 1:10-12*), Paul shows unique gifts serve Christ (*Ephesians 2:10*).

Eddie thought he couldn't shine. *1 Corinthians* shifts: God crafted you distinctly. This builds **Claim Your Lane**: Own your space, trusting God's design. Your niche crowns your cord. A niche makes you an expert.

Case Study: Chris Cortazzo – The Niche Nudge (Malibu)

Chris Cortazzo walked Malibu's shore in 2023, sand gritty and hot between his toes, the Pacific's roar pounding his ears like a drumline in full swing. Leads scattered like seashells—he could chase all comers—but he picked surfers, their sun-bleached hair glinting in the afternoon light as he pitched a $400,000 bungalow. Salt spray stung his lips, sharp and alive, as they leaned in, boards tucked under their arms, the wood weathered and smooth. His voice cut through the crash of waves, steady as a tide, and they nodded. Five months into real estate, 20 broad pitches flopped. Surfers finally signed, closing for $6,000. The deal closed fast as a riptide pulling under, escrow papers crisp with the faint tang of sea air clinging to them. The commission landed, a cool rush like diving into surf, his niche cemented. "I thought broad was best," Chris said, the horizon blazing gold as he stood ankle-deep in foam, "but niche made me king– it's my crown." The waves crashed approval as he grinned, sand still dusting his heels. Chris hit $8 billion by 2024 (U.S. News, 2023).

Eddie's phone sat silent, but Rita rose: "Own your space." He picked condos—a call back: "That's my fit." The $720,000 condo sold for $10,800 on October 15, 2024 (Bay Area MLS, 2024). His cord shone.

Chapter 7: Building a Team

The seventh strand of your Thrive Cord COLLABORATION.

On October 25, 2024, Eddie hunched at the kitchen table, his solo grind draining, papers untouched, savings at $130 after a utility bill. "I can do it alone," Eddie muttered, sinking. Rita recalls Diana leaning on neighbors to fix that flooded rental—hammer clangs blending with the rain's patter, their help lifting her burden. "You're not alone, Trev," she says, her teamwork instinct kicking in, sharp as a chef's call across a bustling kitchen. Ecclesiastes 4:9 fits—Diana's duo outworked solitude, doubling her yield as they patched the roof. Eddie's team can double his return too, lifting him higher than he'd climb alone.

New agents feel isolation's weight, believing God expects solo wins. Eddie bought this lie. *Ecclesiastes 4:9 (NASB)* counters: "Two are better than one because they have a good return for their labor." Written in the 10th century BC (*Ecclesiastes 1:1-3*),

Solomon shows teamwork's advantage (*Genesis 2:18, Mark 6:7*). Collaboration multiplies success.

Eddie thought independence was ideal and collaboration was weakness. *Ecclesiastes* shifts: God designed community. This shapes **Link Arms to Rise**: Trust teamwork to double your haul. Collaboration strengthens your cord and multiplies success. Two lift higher—find your crew.

Case Study: Mark Choey – The Team Triumph (San Jose)

Mark Choey sat in a San Jose loft in 2010, the Silicon Valley buzz humming through the open window like a hive alive with bees, his solo grind a dull ache in his bones. Three months into real estate, 15 solo pitches flopped. He teamed with a mentor, fingers flying over a keyboard that clacked like chopping knives on a board, the air thick with the bitter warmth of coffee and the faint metallic whiff of solder from nearby tech shops. His mentor's "Let's do this" spurred a joint $800,000 condo pitch, their voices syncing like a well-timed kitchen brigade, the buyer's nod a quiet drumroll. The escrow office glowed with neon's flicker, the walls vibrating with the city's pulse as they signed, the commission landing like a warm jolt of espresso down a tired throat. "I thought solo was my strength," Mark said, the tech hum still ringing in his ears as he stood taller, "but teamwork soared—HighNote was born from that lift." closing for $12,000. "Teamwork soared," Mark said, building a $20 million firm by 2024 (AgentAdvice, 2024).

Eddie's breath labored, but Rita grinned: "You're not alone." He called a friend, closed a $780,000 deal, splitting $11,700 on November 10, 2024 (Bay Area MLS, 2024). His cord bound tight. Together wins, every time.

Chapter 8: Staying the Course

The eighth strand is of your Thrive Cord is ENDURANCE.

On November 20, 2024, fog chilled as Eddie's client backs out and he slumps on the porch steps, a client's "I'm out" text glowing. Defeat heavy as a cold oven after a failed bake. Savings at $120 after a car repair. Rita recalled Diana's darkest year—rain on a tarp-covered rental, tenants vanished, rain pattering on a tarp-covered roof with a relentless tap, her whispered prayers blending with the drip-drip into a bucket half-full of muddy water. "Keep going, Eddie," Rita says, her stamina honed by late-night market extended hours. Galatians 6:9 steadies her—Diana didn't lose heart through that flood, reaping a home that stood firm; Eddie's harvest waits too, if he presses on without growing weary. "I should quit," Eddie whispered. Rita smiles, "Diana's flood—or my overtime—same grit, same gain."

Setbacks tempt new agents to quit, suggesting God bails. Eddie believed this. *Galatians 6:9 (NASB)* counters: "Let us not lose heart in doing good, for in due time we will reap if we do not grow weary." Written around 49AD (*Galatians 1:6-9*), Paul promises harvest through grit (*Genesis 6, Hebrews 12:2*).

Eddie thought losses ended him. *Galatians* shifts: **God ensures you reap if you stay**. This forms **Stay in for the Win**: Trust God's timing through setbacks. Endurance holds your cord. Endurance reaps rewards.

Case Study: Joyce Rey – The Open House Win (San Francisco)

Joyce Rey stood under a dripping umbrella in Pacific Heights, fog curling around Victorian eaves like smoke from a dying fire, rain pelting the cobblestones with a relentless tap-tap that soaked her shoes. Her open house for a $500,000 home drew one couple, their boots squelching on the mat as they stepped in, the musty air warming as she lit a fire, the crackling logs spitting sparks. Slow months had gnawed at her—quitting beckoned like a soft bed after a long shift—but she stayed, her voice soft as the embers' glow, guiding them through. They bought, the escrow's ink drying with a satisfying snap, the commission landing like a warm ember in her hands, its heat a quiet triumph. "No turnout felt like failure," Joyce said, the fog still clinging to her coat as she locked the door, "but persistence won—$6 billion later, it's my proof." The rain kept falling, but she stood taller. "Grit won," Joyce said, hitting $6 billion by 2024 (RealTrends, 2024).

Eddie slumped, but Rita gripped his arm: "Keep going." He called back—a yes. The $800,000 deal closed for $12,000 on December 5, 2024 (Bay Area MLS, 2024). His cord steadied. Endurance turns losses to wins—stay in.

Chapter 9: Nurturing Relationships

The ninth strand of your Thrive Cord is CONNECTION.

On December 15, 2024, Eddie's kitchen table creaked, his energy like a flat soufflé left too long chasing new leads, old contacts ignored. Rita recalls Diana's friends—loyalty born from kimchi chats and laughter over steaming bowls. "Tend your roots, Eddie," she says, her voice calm but firm, like a chef plating wisdom. He knocks again—success blooms, a past client's smile warm as fresh bread. Proverbs 27:17 sharpens it—Diana's regulars honed her edge, keeping her sharp through lean years; Eddie's past clients will hone his too, building strength through trust. Roots bloom big—nurture them.

New agents overlook past ties, believing God forgets them. Eddie bought this lie. *Proverbs 27:17 (NASB)* counters: "Iron sharpens iron, so one man sharpens another." Written in the 10th century BC (*Proverbs 1:1*), Solomon shows connection hones (*Ruth 1, 2 Timothy 1:2*).

Eddie thought old ties were dead. *Proverbs* shifts: God builds through roots. This crafts **Tend Your Roots**: Trust relationships to bloom. Connection enriches your cord. Past relationships yield gold.

Case Study: Matt Altman – The Referral Gold (Palm Springs)

Matt Altman walked a Palm Springs street in 2023, desert sage wafting sharp and green in the dry air, the sun glinting off mid-century glass like a polished blade slicing through dusk. Slow months parched him, a drought of deals—new leads felt like mirages. His brother's "Call them" spurred a note to a past client after two lost deals. He scribbled a $50 note to a past client, the paper crisp under his pen, its scratch a quiet promise in the stillness. Handed over, it lingered with the heat's low hum, sage brushing his knuckles, then exploded—a $1.2M referral landed, the buyer's voice crackling through the phone like a fire catching. The teacher's son referred a $1.2M deal, earning $18,000. The escrow office buzzed with ceiling fans, the contract's pages fluttering as he signed, the commission a rich sip of cool water on a cracked tongue. "I thought new leads were all that mattered," Matt said, sand still dusting his shoes as he grinned, "but old paid bigger"— Matt said, thriving at Altman Brothers (AgentAdvice, 2024).

Eddie's notebook dusted, but Rita nodded: "Tend your roots." He texted an old lead—a referral. The $850,000 deal closed for $12,750 on January 5, 2025 (Bay Area MLS, 2025). His cord glowed gold.

Conclusion

Eddie stands tall on that same porch, the evening air cool against his skin, Diana's legacy pulsing in his veins like a heartbeat he can feel. Zdenek's gravel-crunching note, Beckie's salt-kissed reel, Elisa's sawdust-stung flip, Tracy's heel-clicking focus, Chris's wave-crashing niche, Mark's espresso-jolt teamwork, Joyce's rain-soaked grit, Matt's sage-scented gold—each strand weaves a cord of courage, focus, and endurance. Diana's journey—from Korea's ash and bombs to a coffee-jar starter—lit their path, and now Eddie's ember burns bright, a new agent ready to thrive. Your path's set too—nine wins, nine lessons, one cord. Weave it strong.

Your cord's woven: nine lessons, one lifeline.

Here they are, your strength:

- **Courage** – *Joshua 1:9*: "Be strong and courageous… for the Lord your God is with you…"
- **Perseverance** – *Romans 5:3-4*: "Tribulation brings about perseverance…"
- **Gratitude** – *Zechariah 4:10*: "Do not despise these small beginnings…"

- **Resourcefulness** – *Matthew 13:31-32*: "The kingdom of heaven is like a mustard seed…"
- **Focus** – *Proverbs 16:3*: "Commit your works to the Lord…"
- **Identity** – *1 Corinthians 12:4-5*: "Varieties of gifts, but the same Spirit…"
- **Collaboration** – *Ecclesiastes 4:9*: "Two are better than one…"
- **Endurance** – *Galatians 6:9*: "Let us not lose heart in doing good…"
- **Connection** – *Proverbs 27:17*: "Iron sharpens iron…"

Pull it tight—your year one awaits.

Call to Action

You've walked Eddie's path, felt Diana's grit, tasted my wisdom. Don't let your ember fade.

Start by adding the accompanying THRIVE workbook.

Enroll in our California Association of REALTORS© approved newly licensed agent training class.(www.car.org) Turn nine strands into nine weeks of growth.

Next, our bi-monthly coaching and mentoring on-line class, puts us by your side, like Diana was for us.

The elite mastermind includes global travel, meeting with like-minded, kingdom builder agents, brokers and investors to network and fellowship. Ensure your passport and global entry cards are up to date.

Your year one begins today.

- **Chapter 1**: Ready to tighten your courage? Weave it now.

- **Chapter 2**: Ready to forge perseverance? Turn "no" into strength.

- **Chapter 3**: Ready to spark gratitude? Value your ember.

- **Chapter 4**: Ready to plant roots? Grow from little.

- **Chapter 5**: Ready to carve focus? Sharpen your path.

- **Chapter 6**: Ready to find your lane? Crown your identity.

- **Chapter 7**: Ready to build your team? Lift together.

- **Chapter 8**: Ready to stay the course? Reap your harvest.

- **Chapter 9**: Ready to nurture roots? Bloom your gold.

About the Author

Annette DiResta is a real estate powerhouse whose 25-year career in residential and commercial real estate is a testament to resilience, grit, and transformative success. Inspired by her mother Diana's escape from war-torn Korea and rise from a tip-jar income to a legacy of strength, Annette channels that same tenacity into empowering newly licensed agents. Through her acclaimed training with the California Association of REALTORS©, she equips aspiring real estate professionals with the tools to turn challenges into thriving careers.

Annette's journey began in Honolulu, where early roles at KITV and American Airlines honed her discipline and adaptability. After raising her children in Silicon Valley, she entered real estate as an assistant to top producers Jim Church and Nori Shiba at Coldwell Banker Morgan Hill. Her relentless drive propelled her to Top Producer status, earning the prestigious International Diamond Society designation and certification as a Property Previews Specialist for luxury properties.

Securing her Broker's license, Annette joined Alain Pinel REALTORS© (now Compass) as a Broker

Associate, where she again claimed Top Producer honors and a place in the elite President's Circle. Her expertise expanded with certifications as a Relocation of the World Specialist, National Association of REALTORS© Certified International Property Specialist (CIPS), At Home with Diversity (AHWD), and Senior Real Estate Specialist (SRES). She later founded HI CARE BROKER—Hawaii California Real Estate Broker—and Morgan Hill Real Estate, serving clients across the Pacific Coast with a Santa Clara County Green Designation and federal certifications for government contracts.

Rooted in her diverse heritage—raised in a military family with ties to Korea, Taiwan, and Germany—Annette's commitment to community shines. She played a pivotal role in launching Cathedral of Faith Morgan Hill and Vive Morgan Hill, and secured a Conditional Use Permit for Jubilee Bridge Church. A Leadership Morgan Hill alum, she mentors at the University of Colorado Boulder and served on the Santa Clara County San Martin Planning Advisory Committee. Her decade-long volunteer work at Lucile Packard Children's Hospital (now Stanford Children's Hospital), along with support for events like the Morgan Hill Marathon and National Senior Olympics, reflects her servant's heart.

Faith is Annette's cornerstone. From teaching children's Bible studies to serving on church council and production teams, she has advocated for leasing spaces—like converting a 25,000 sq ft Gold's Gym into a sanctuary for Jubilee Bridge. In April 2025, she embarked on her first High Impact Missions| HypeCon with Vive Church (formerly C3SV) trip to Dubai, UAE, advancing her mission to serve globally.

Through *Thrive in Year One*, Annette distills her expertise into a roadmap for new agents, blending practical strategies with her inspiring story. As the Co-Founder of The DiResta Group, alongside her son Trevor, she continues to build empires and advance her faith-driven mission. Discover her classes and mastermind at www.morganhill.realestate or www.thedirestagroup.realestate, and join a legacy of turning dreams into reality.

Acknowledgments

To Abba, Jesus Christ, and the Holy Spirit—my Lord and Savior, anchor, navigator, inspiration.

To my Pastors at Vive (formerly C3SV), Jubilee, New Hope, Cathedral of Faith, Generations Foursquare—your spiritual teachings strengthened and humbled me to be a servant leader.

To Leadership Morgan Hill—leadership inspired community service.

To Lorna Hines—my coach, admonishing me to never leave money on the table.

To the University of Colorado Boulder—my heart, memories and mentorship fuel.

To Isaiah Grant—Kingdom Impact extracted these books out of me.

To Faith Driven Entrepreneur, FDE Investor and Overflow—keys of generosity.

To NAR, CAR, SCCAOR, SFAR, HICENTRAL, Lone Wolf, ORT, Supraekey—your platforms fueled my passionate career with its challenges and rewards.

To every reader, every agent daring to thrive—your wins are my joy.

Glossary

- **Commission**: A fee, typically 3-6% of a property's sale price, paid to the agent for facilitating a transaction (National Association of REALTORS©, 2024).
- **Escrow**: A neutral third-party process holding funds and documents until a real estate transaction's conditions are met (National Association of REALTORS©, 2024).
- **Listing**: An agreement between a seller and agent to market a property for sale (California Association of REALTORS©, 2023).
- **Top Producer**: An agent recognized for exceptional sales performance by their brokerage (Coldwell Banker, 2024).
- **Certified International Property Specialist (CIPS)**: A National Association of REALTORS© designation for expertise in international real estate transactions (National Association of REALTORS©, 2024).

- **At Home with Diversity (AHWD)**: A National Association of REALTORS© certification for serving diverse clients (National Association of REALTORS, 2023).
- **Seniors Real Estate Specialist© (SRES©)**: A National Association of REALTORS© designation to better serve homebuyers and sellers ages 50 and over.

Index

- **Courage, Zdenek Tronicek**
- **Perseverance, Jason Barry**
- **Gratitude, Beckie Nielson**
- **Resourcefulness, Elisa Covington**
- **Focus, Tracy Tutor**
- **Identity, Chris Cortazzo**
- **Collaboration, Mark Choey**
- **Endurance, Joyce Rey**
- **Connection, Matt Altman**
- **Scriptures**:
  - *Joshua 1:9*, 9
  - *Romans 5:3-4*,
  - *Zechariah 4:10*
  - *Matthew 13:31-32*
  - *Proverbs 16:3*
  - *1 Corinthians 12:4-5*
  - *Ecclesiastes 4:9*

    - *Galatians 6:9*
    - *Proverbs 27:17*
- **Coaching, Counseling, Mastermind**
- **Thrive Cord**

APA Citations

- AgentAdvice. (2024). *Real estate agent success stories*. https://agentadvice.com/success-stories/
- Bay Area MLS. (2024). *San Francisco real estate transactions, Q2-Q4 2024*. https://www.bayareamls.com/data
- Bay Area MLS. (2025). *San Francisco real estate transactions, Q1 2025*. https://www.bayareamls.com/data
- California Association of Realtors. (2023). *Real estate terminology guide*. https://www.car.org/knowledge-center/glossary
- Coldwell Banker. (2024). *Agent recognition programs*. https://www.coldwellbanker.com/for-agents/recognition
- Hollywood Reporter. (2023, June 15). *Million Dollar Listing stars share secrets*. https://www.hollywoodreporter.com/tv/tv-features/million-dollar-listing-stars-secrets-1235512345/
- Keener, C. S. (1999). *A commentary on the Gospel of Matthew*. Eerdmans Publishing. https://www.eerdmans.com/Products/Books/9780802838215.aspx

- National Association of Realtors. (2023). *At Home with Diversity (AHWD) certification*. https://www.nar.realtor/education/designations-and-certifications/ahwd
- National Association of Realtors. (2024). *Certified International Property Specialist (CIPS) designation*. https://www.nar.realtor/education/designations-and-certifications/cips
- National Association of Realtors. (2024). *Real estate transaction glossary*. https://www.nar.realtor/resources/real-estate-glossary
- National Association of Realtors. (2024). *Understanding real estate commissions*. https://www.nar.realtor/for-members/commissions
- New Silver. (2023). *Flipping success stories*. https://newsilver.com/success-stories/
- RealTrends. (2024). *America's top real estate professionals*. https://realtrends.com/rankings/americas-top-real-estate-professionals/
- The Lockman Foundation. (1995). *New American Standard Bible*. https://www.lockman.org/new-american-standard-bible-nasb/
- U.S. News & World Report. (2023, May 20). *Top real estate agents in Malibu*.

https://realestate.usnews.com/agents/malibu-top-agents

www.ingramcontent.com/pod-product-compliance
Lightning Source LLC
Chambersburg PA
CBHW041203230426
43673CB00035B/500